M000303564

A ROMANCE
OF EAST AND WEST

A Romance of East and West

◆ Al-Byout ◆

Interiors by Mona Hajj

WRITTEN WITH JUDITH NASATIR
FOREWORD BY WILLIAM ABRANOWICZ

THE MONACELLI PRESS

CONTENTS

FOREWORD

Ansel Adams once said, "If I can get excited about a place, I can make a good photograph of it." There are certain things that really excite me: the presence of geologic time in the landscapes of Africa and the Middle East, the ornate architecture and interiors of Europe and Asia, the raw history of the United States. The patina of time and the traces of man's historical hand stimulate my eye, tell me stories, and touch my heart. Adams's excitement, I believe, refers to this heightened awareness of a place, transcending the five senses, and connecting the individual—in this case, the artist—to something bigger. Something inexplicable that I try to explain through images.

The workings of nature levy their own magnetic pull. I never quite understood Frank Gehry's work until I was photographing the Disney Center in Los Angeles and a storm passed overhead. The skin of the building breathed with the darkening sky, pulsing and changing shape to mirror the sky's movements. The then-new building was in constant, fluent dialogue with the ancient and immutable forces of nature.

In photographing an interior, the history presented in the objects or furniture; the walls themselves; the stories, real or imagined result in images that are meaningful. That is when a room transcends mere decoration. In these types of places, the transience of modern life is escaped and forgotten. It becomes irrelevant.

To most any photographer, time is masterful at creating beauty, and Mona Hajj is a master of time. The elements of time that Mona grasps and the soft patina she creates with it are full-blown cinematic, lush, and colorful—dare I say, Romantic (with a capital R)? I am talking of the visual romance of the films of Merchant and Ivory—one beautiful thing after another. It is not the work of a set decorator but rather of a serious observer journeying and taking us through the exotic and making it recognizable. For Mona, the elements of a room—the rugs, the abundant layers of European, African, Asian, or Middle Eastern textiles, the sensual curves of furniture she designs or antiques she brings are voluptuously upholstered in mysteriously rich brocades or velvets, and the collections of ancient pottery and art combine like alchemy to form new but magically familiar stories that comfort and hold you.

Like Albert Bierstadt, the Hudson River School artist whose work Mona cherishes, she takes the best elements of nature, light, humanity, history, craft, and depth and works them into a wonderfully idyllic version of sanctuary creating a place that could only be described as Home (with a capital H).

—William Abranowicz

INTRODUCTION

Beautiful. Exotic. Serene. Complex. Romantic. Instinctive. Learned. These words describe the world I come from, and the way I want the homes—in Arabic, *al byout*—I design to feel. I grew up in Beirut, Lebanon, in rooms made lush, warm, and sumptuous with layers of rugs and textiles and a mix of furnishings, art, and decorative objects from all different eras. Many of the pieces we lived with had been handed down through the family over the generations. There were no formulas for the way these rooms came together, which may explain why I am so averse to any sort of design formula now. They were full of things we loved and others had loved before us. In this way, these objects came to embody our stories and memories. Antiquities were everywhere in our view, in the arts and artifacts of our culture displayed in the streets and structures of Beirut. In what had endured we could see the ebbs and flows of empires and the continuous absorption of influences through trade and travel, from the arrival of the mysterious Phoenicians through to the present.

This rich history has put the world today into a unique perspective for me. As a child, I took the art, architecture, and the layers of history for granted. No longer. When I came to Baltimore as a teenager, I learned that anything one hundred years old was considered "antique." It took me time to adapt to that definition of age. In many families who share my origins, we live with things that are many hundreds of years old, even a thousand or more.

East and West are very much married in my work, my aesthetic, and my worldview, just as they are in the evolution of visual culture when you take the longest possible view. I am comfortable with both because I am so aware of how the past informs the present every time we reinvent it. I also know that what we are conditioned to think of as separate—the East and the West—have overlapped all through the history of the known world, from the ancient Egyptian and Persian Empires to the Greeks, the Romans, and onward. There has always been a romance between East and West. As the known world has expanded, the West has repeatedly discovered, absorbed, and reinterpreted the various visual cultures of the East in successive periods of exoticism. Much of what we are taught to think of as a form of renaissance involves adapting an older idea from one culture to the contemporary sensibility of another. This is true even in the nineteenth and twentieth centuries. I am very attracted to the designs of Louis Comfort Tiffany, for example, who was inspired by Morocco early on. The work of William Morris holds great appeal, but the roots of his patterns are the organic, which is the visual language of my native culture. I grew up with all these patterns. That is one reason why I love carpets so much and use them as the foundation of every room I create. Truly, design is amazing.

In the culture of the East, homes tend to be inviting and comfortable, tactile, and warm. I still have memories of my grandmother's house, and not because it was grand. It was very simple but very warm. We never wanted to leave once we were there. The rooms were filled with pieces that were just thrown together. There was no real rhyme or reason behind the choices or the groupings, but everything felt so right. In one hallway she had a beautiful armoire from Turkey that she used for our clothes. In my mind, it was huge, but I am sure that is because I was small. I remember how masculine it was, which was not the usual. Next to it sat a small chair, covered in a textile full of flowers. Her bed was so very appealing. It smelled good. It looked good. It had the most wonderful pillows, a collection she had inherited. I cannot recall the colors of the living room, but it was always so cushy. My grandparents and parents never thought about whether a certain piece would fit or not. If it felt right to them, they used it. These experiences gave me liberty to create spaces in the same way. I love all the pieces individually. I never make a hard and fast plan, although I always know what kind of thing I need, and where it will go. But I take what I have in my studio and in storage that suits the individual client, knowing I will find whatever else we may need. This is why I believe that if it feels good, it is good. And it works.

Visiting Beirut and Europe each year to see family, I looked, shopped, and shipped pieces back to Baltimore from everywhere I went. Now I use the Internet much more, but I still buy only what I love through dealers with whom I have already developed a relationship or who come recommended by a trusted source. Even when a client is looking, the piece has to be something special.

For so many reasons, I find the Islamic decorative arts—and especially the textiles, pottery and glass, carpets, stone, copper, and other metalwork of the eighth through twelfth centuries— amazing. The works from this period have a unique intricacy and depth. These pieces command the eye and reward each viewing with a new discovery. Even when the designs are simple, they have great depth and many layers. Not all of them are religious, as people in the West tend to think. There is a great deal of secular art, too. But what matters is that the artists of this era are truly masters of their form. Ornament abounds, yet it is very discreet. The potency of the colors is

OPPOSITE: Pieces of tenth-, eleventh-, and twelfth-century Persian
pottery with an eighteenth-century Turkish architectural
view, pages from an eighteenth-century Koran, and a Tang horse.

marvelous. The calligraphy is so artistic in its line, so inventive in its design and pattern, so immediately communicative on an intellectual, emotional, and spiritual level simultaneously. Islamic architecture takes this idea into three dimensions. The exteriors tend to be extremely simple, but the interiors are poetic—full of ornament and decorated on practically every surface. You are there and you wonder. Islamic art doesn't glorify the individual artist, with very rare exceptions. It emphasizes the team. Always. What matters above all is where something came from and the quality of its workmanship.

I love so many things about the West, and I am truly passionate about English, European, Asian, Russian, Swedish, and American furniture, decorative arts, and fine arts. I find the marriage of English and European furnishings from the eighteenth, nineteenth, and twentieth centuries with textiles from the East to be particularly fascinating. And I am enamored especially with the clarity and sensibility of modern architecture: the cleanliness, the precision, the simplicity. Juxtaposing something very old with something very minimalist, something very exotic with something very familiar makes sense to me emotionally, intellectually, and visually. The contrast underscores that, in spite of everything that suggests the opposite, culture in the broadest sense is continuity. Nothing happens out of the blue. Some people think we are inventing new designs. We are, but only very rarely. We are just evolving. And borrowing from geniuses of the past. Let us give all our predecessors a great deal of credit.

I delight in seeing how one group folds into another when I travel. The conversation with the past and the future is continuous. Works of art and objects that live through time and endure—all the old things from around the world that make us marvel, including the century-old brownstone that is home to my design studio, the Persian rugs that I adore, the Baltimore silver and English porcelain that I collect—all begin with quality. On quality, I cannot compromise. When I fall in love with a piece, I know I will eventually find a home for it. I also know the attraction is more than simply a visceral response to beauty. It also encompasses functionality, for good design involves both. The same is true with homes. We can live in the most beautiful place, but if it does not work for us, what good is it? My goal is to create interiors that people really want to be in, and live in, once they come through the door—rooms that marry sensuality with sensibility with personality, and made soft, inviting, and comfortable with layer upon layer of beauty. I am happiest when the place I deliver to my clients is a place they look forward to coming home to.

OPPOSITE: New, sumptuous silk velvet with a mid-eighteenth-century Moroccan silk panel and an Indonesian silk textile.

RUGS:
THE FOUNDATION

I am enamored with rugs. I grew up surrounded by them. My family rarely threw a carpet away (or, really, anything else they loved). If they liked a new one, they would layer it over another that was already in place. If they wanted to change the look of a piece of furniture, they would simply throw a carpet on top of it. For me, rugs are the foundation of the room. I start with them and build from there. The one absolute is authenticity, which is why relationships with trustworthy dealers are essential.

As I begin searching for the rugs for a house, I have a sense of the types and styles that will best suit the client and the rooms. Whether antique or contemporary, knotted or flat woven, from the East or from the West or both, this vision interconnects the color palette, the intricacy and scale of the pattern, and the texture and depth of the pile in a particular poetry and harmony. Should a truly beautiful rug capture my heart but differ from what I had imagined, I will make it work as long as it seems right for the client and creates a base for the given room. From room to room, I want the rugs to share a vocabulary of tones. I prefer for them to work together organically so the sequence will not jar the eye as it moves from space to space.

The size of the rug is certainly very important, but for me it is not the determining factor for choosing this element of the room. If one rug does not fit, I will put down another with it to make up the difference. Suppose the dining room is 30 feet long, and the rug that appeals is only 24 feet. To extend it to 28 feet, if that's what is necessary, I will find another rug I love in the same coloration and layer the two. This works better in a large room; in tighter spaces, it can overwhelm. But if a corner of that room—or any room—calls for special attention, I will highlight it with its own carpet, even if it overlaps the main one. The effect is always richer and more interesting. There are no hard and fast rules, apart from my commitment to give the best of my expertise.

OPPOSITE: In this Chevy Chase, Maryland, front hallway, a Caucasian kilim,
c. 1880, grounds an early twentieth-century English sofa with pillows made from
a mid-nineteenth-century Turkish man's robe and verdure tapestries.
OVERLEAF: Facing the sofa is an early twentieth-century Spanish table. By the stairs,
a Persian calligraphy candle from the 1900s sits atop two nineteenth-century trunks.

PRECEDING SPREAD: In this Washington, D.C., dining room, a Persian sarouk, c. 1920s, defines the dining area. Layered over it at one end is an early twentieth-century Karaja rug. A late nineteenth-century American sideboard flanked by Biedermeier chairs balances the original fireplace mantel. A footed Persian bowl, a mid-eighteenth-century painted mirror, and a nineteenth-century bell jar chandelier complete the mix. ABOVE: In this San Francisco hallway, the colors of nautical paintings by J. S. Johnston complement the early twentieth-century Serab runner. An eighteenth-century giltwood mirror gives the space a focal point. OPPOSITE: A Khotan carpet from the 1900s draws attention to one end of this Los Angeles living room. Since it was far too small to carpet the entire floor, we laid it on top of a late nineteenth-century Sultanabad rug. Late nineteenth-century French fauteuils flank a George III mahogany tea table in front of an Elger Esser cityscape.

RIGHT: This early twentieth-century Baltimore house had retained much of its original detailing, including paneling and molding. A bold Karabagh runner from the Caucasus balances the paneling while the mahogany frame of the George III sofa keeps the wood tone consistent. Mirrors above Anglo-Indian console tables create symmetry without matching.
OVERLEAF: A luxuriant European silk, c. 1880, I found on my travels covers the center table in the living room, where an early seventeenth-century Ushak sets the tone. A Cy Twombly lithograph on the mantel feels right with a group of ancient pots from Latin America and Asia.

PRECEDING SPREAD: In another seating area in the living room, early twentieth-century Louis XVI–style armchairs flank a custom tufted sofa. The small side table combines a late seventeenth-century William and Mary box on a turned stand. ABOVE: With an antique Shivan carpet to add warmth, a comfortable chair, a nineteenth-century tripod table, and a turn-of-the-twentieth-century French breakfront, this Washington, D.C., foyer becomes a welcoming place to sit, read, or wait for a moment. OPPOSITE: The light in the Bradley Stevens painting inspired the decor of this very feminine room. A late nineteenth-century Aubusson carpet and a Murano chandelier play off the color palette. Next to the desk, engravings of furniture details, c. 1750, layer in more history.

In many parts of the world, rugs are movable treasures that convey cultural heritage and family legacy. Families often pass them from one generation to the next. For those who know and appreciate them, rugs provide entrée into a world of information, tradition, and artistry. They relate a story of place and culture through a form of functional beauty. As a general rule, each style of rug bears the name of its country or region of origin. This is perhaps even more true in the rug-making regions in Asia, the Middle East, and around the Mediterranean. Consider Isfahan, Anatolian, or Kashan as just three examples. When a style of exceptionally high quality emerges within a given rug type, it often gains a distinguishing appellation. Kashan is a case in point. Most rugs from this region are known simply as Kashans. But there are also the much rarer, much more formal "Mohtasham" Kashans. In Farsi, "Mohtasham" means "Magnificent." These rugs truly are that, with incredibly potent and exotic colors and patterns so intricate they almost defy belief. Their fronts and backs are virtually indistinguishable because the knots are so dense and clearly defined.

In my view, Persian rugs are supreme among the many types of carpets made in the East. Because so much of the world has long prized their artistry, they offer a natural point of engagement for different cultures and their varying aesthetics. I love Turkish carpets and Ushaks as well, which are less visually intense. Nomadic carpets—kilims and other flat weaves—are also favorites. In these, the pattern dominates. The desert peoples wove these rugs for many practical purposes: as soft walls and decorative hangings, as runners and cloths for the table, as padding or blankets for horses and camels, even as bags. They were multi-functional from the start. It feels natural to honor their history and tradition by using them in this way today.

PRECEDING SPREAD: A modern sofa harmonizes with traditional furnishings in this serene Los Angeles living room. A late nineteenth-century Sultanabad from Central Persia lays a foundation of understated pattern. A collection of French faience draws the eye up from the French limestone mantel. An Ushak rug, c. 1910, covers the serpentine back of the nineteenth-century sofa. OPPOSITE AND OVERLEAF: A Persian Sarouk rug, c. 1880, sets the stage for this Los Angeles dining room. A Jansen chandelier, c. 1940s, reflects light in all directions. The sideboard dates to the late eighteenth century. The eggshell background of the curtain fabric is distinctive, but does not contrast sharply with the white walls. An Art Deco vitrine, c. 1920, serves as a china cabinet.

ABOVE AND OPPOSITE: When space permits, foyers can be made welcoming instead of just spaces to pass through. In this San Francisco apartment, a Persian Tabriz carpet, c. 1880, creates an inviting feeling with a late eighteenth-century secretary-bookcase, a late eighteenth-century gilt girandole mirror, and a nineteenth-century Syrian mother-of-pearl chair. At the opposite end, a mid-seventeenth-century Flemish verdure tapestry is a dramatic focal point. Art Deco lounge chairs offer comfortable perches. OVERLEAF: An early twentieth-century French gilt-metal chandelier, an eighteenth-century rustic ranch table repurposed as a coffee table, a nineteenth-century mahogany canterbury, and a Tabriz rug, c. 1900, from northwest Persia give this Los Angeles family room a casual, comfortable, collected feel.

ABOVE AND OPPOSITE: The kitchen is designed as a room for gathering and casual dining. A late nineteenth-century Moghan Kazak runner gives a foundation of tradition; midcentury suspension lights add modernist notes. For the island, I retrofitted a nineteenth-century carved-oak side cabinet. In the window bay, a nine-teenth-century extendable French farm table seats ten on French bamboo chairs and a built-in banquette.

ABOVE AND OPPOSITE: Small spaces like this 8-by-10-foot room in San Francisco become functional and comfortable for intimate gatherings with furnishings of the right scale. A Persian Laver Kirman rug, c. 1880, serves as a base for a nineteenth-century American painted blanket chest and a late eighteenth-century mahogany side table. The Bay view inspired the palette of soft blues.

FOR THOSE WHO KNOW AND
APPRECIATE THEM, RUGS
PROVIDE ENTRÉE INTO A WORLD
OF INFORMATION, TRADITION,
AND ARTISTRY. THEY RELATE
A STORY OF PLACE AND
CULTURE THROUGH A FORM
OF FUNCTIONAL BEAUTY.

OPPOSITE: In a Washington, D.C., breakfast room, a vintage, hand-woven Persian carpet with a simple, geometric stripe establishes the basis for a quiet design that makes the most of the luxurious natural light. A Neolithic Chinese pottery vessel creates a wonderful centerpiece for a pedestal table of reclaimed pine.

RIGHT: A custom paint color, faux-finished cabinets, a farm sink, and stainless-steel appliances give this Washington, D.C., kitchen the sensibility of much-loved, older space reinterpreted for today.

ABOVE AND OPPOSITE: Rugs bring warmth and beauty to every room in the house, including kitchens and baths. In this San Francisco house, a late nineteenth-century English needlepoint rug in the kitchen echoes a feature wall of early twentieth-century handmade Tunisian tiles. A custom panel of glass rondels screens the bath window; an Indian plaque of mirrored glass and white tile adds interest over the bathtub. The vanity is a retrofitted nineteenth-century cabinet.

RIGHT: A late nineteenth-century Bidjar carpet from central Persia sets the stage for an L-shaped sofa that was key to the design of this Washington, D.C., family room. It had to fit the space proportionally. More important, it had to be large enough for the entire family and friends to gather around the TV hidden inside the cabinet.
OVERLEAF: The second-floor landing of this Los Angeles house is large enough to accommodate a comfortable seating area defined by a nineteenth-century Bakshaish rug from northern Persia. A nineteenth-century French chandelier hangs over the stairwell.

JUXTAPOSING SOMETHING
VERY OLD WITH SOMETHING VERY
MINIMALIST, SOMETHING VERY
EXOTIC WITH SOMETHING
VERY FAMILIAR MAKES SENSE TO ME
EMOTIONALLY, INTELLECTUALLY,
AND VISUALLY. THE CONTRAST
UNDERSCORES THAT, IN SPITE OF
EVERYTHING THAT SUGGESTS
THE OPPOSITE, CULTURE IN THE
BROADEST SENSE IS CONTINUITY.

OPPOSITE: The airy, small-scale pattern of the rug in this lady's dressing room lays a base for a light and graceful atmosphere. Extending from the dressing room into the master bedroom, the fabric-and-lace-covered walls pick up on the rug's delicacy to create a feminine spirit, without being cloying. The marble-topped bookcase is a Jansen piece from 1940.

ABOVE: Artwork and a properly scaled chair or two can transform even comparatively narrow hallways into more than simple transitional spaces. An early eighteenth-century Greek embroidered textile provides a marvelous background for nineteenth-century Regency hall chairs and a mid-nine-teenth-century inlaid Syrian table. OPPOSITE: This passageway was perfect for creating an intimate seating area for small family gatherings or just a quiet hour of reading. A late nineteenth-century Persian Bidjar rug underlays a c. 1920 Syrian coffee table and wood and mother-of-pearl Syrian side tables, c. 1890. Above the sofa are framed fragments of seventh-century Egyptian textiles.

ABOVE AND OPPOSITE: An antique Bessarabian rug provides a layer of warmth,
comfort, and beauty in a guest bedroom. In the hallway outside, carpets
and artwork enhance the experience of passage. While the carpets do not need
to match from one area to the next, they should flow beautifully together.

I FIND THE MARRIAGE OF ENGLISH
AND EUROPEAN FURNISHINGS
FROM THE EIGHTEENTH,
NINETEENTH, AND TWENTIETH
CENTURIES WITH TEXTILES FROM
THE EAST TO BE PARTICULARLY
FASCINATING. AND I AM ENAMORED
ESPECIALLY WITH THE CLARITY
AND SENSIBILITY OF MODERN
ARCHITECTURE: THE CLEANLINESS,
THE PRECISION, THE SIMPLICITY.

OPPOSITE: The custom millwork that lines this gentleman's dressing
room makes use of every available inch, including space above the
window. Adding an exotic note, a nineteenth-century Ottoman
textile with gold thread upholsters the seventeenth-century stool.

TEXTILES:
CREATING A MOOD

I have always loved textiles. I am sure I inherited this passion from my family, who were textile importers. My parents traveled often in search of beautiful designs and reveled in their finds from China, Europe, and all over the Middle East. To this day, working with textiles—choosing, arranging, mixing, hanging, making pillows, throws, table runners, and bed covers—raises my spirits.

Textiles are undervalued as an art form, in my view. Those that I seek out and collect are handmade and sometimes extremely old. They are just as expressive as rugs, for they embody the same kind of human romance. Each fragment, each length of yardage tells the story of how it was made and where.

The intricacy of antique Persian and other Islamic textiles—the weaving, the colors, the patterns—seems completely ingenious to me and without compare. These fabrics tend to be sober in their look and soft on the eye. The workmanship reveals such heart and soul. When two or more people worked on the same textile, the weave often shows the variations in the hand. When an artisan introduced a new batch of wool or silk from a different dye lot, the shade of that color may shift at that point. Sometimes, the vegetable dyes create that inherent deviation. Whether subtle or not, these differences add so much to the character of the piece. To an eye that prizes machined perfection, they may be unexpected at first. I find these marks of the imperfect hand beautiful, and sources of delight and wonder.

All cultures borrow from each other. Textiles document the evidence of that sharing most remarkably. As goods for trading and gifts exchanged between heads of state and other emissaries, they traveled across all the boundaries of the known world. Wherever these beautiful creations arrived, they became objects for emulation. The textiles of the Ottoman Empire offer examples of just how fluid such cross-cultural influences can be over centuries. When the Ottoman Empire was at its height from the eighth to the fifteenth centuries, it encompassed most of Southeast Europe, parts of Central Europe, Western Asia, parts of Eastern Europe and the Caucasus, North Africa, and the Horn of Africa. Under its aegis, culture flowered.

OPPOSITE AND OVERLEAF: In this Washington, D.C., entry, the challenge was to find beautiful pieces that fit the space and would marry together to create a warm embrace of welcome. From the nineteenth-century Uzbekistan Suzani wall hanging to the antique Turkish textiles on the pillows to the Kurdish rug, fabrics play a major role in establishing this mood. A nineteenth-century hand-carved coffer and Regency ebonized bench enrich the spirit.

TEXTILES SOFTEN ANY SPACE.
AT FIRST GLANCE, WE SEE THEIR
BEAUTY. THEN THEIR COLORS,
PATTERNS, AND TEXTURES
ADD INTRIGUE. LIKE ALL WORKS
OF ART AND OBJECTS THAT
LIVE THROUGH TIME AND
ENDURE, FABRICS TEACH US
ABOUT QUALITY. THEY HAVE
SO MANY STORIES TO TELL.

OPPOSITE: An early eighteenth-century Flemish verdure tapestry brings an idea of the outdoors into the core of the interior. OVERLEAF: In this Chevy Chase, Maryland, dining room, a nineteenth-century, gold-embroidered, striped Turkish textile that was once a pair of pasha's pants forms an unexpected backdrop for a work by Milton Avery and an array of ancient pottery on the mantel. A printed Persian fabric panel, c. 1800, runs the length of the table, while a late nine-teenth-century Lavar Kirman rug lays the groundwork. Sixteenth-century Spanish tiles on the side table insert additional small jolts of color and pattern.

I am always looking. And I am always amazed by what I see. I love Persian textiles, Syrian textiles, Turkish textiles, and so many others from the regions of the Middle East and around the Mediterranean. Sometimes it can be very difficult to differentiate one from another. Only with a foundation of knowledge and the kind of expertise that comes from continuously working with these materials can one begin to recognize that this piece was made in Ankara and this one in Istanbul. That this one is Syrian. Or that this one is Persian. The same is true with textiles from other parts of the world. France or England, China or Italy, America or Latin America, Africa, India, and more—every region of the world weaves its rich history into its fabrics. When chosen with deliberation and care, they can work so very well to create the desired mood within a room and a home. One great dividing line, however, is the content of the ornamentation: the arts from the Islamic countries never represent human beings, while those from the Western countries so often do.

Antique and vintage textiles from all corners of the world tend to be cotton, linen, silk, or wool, so they feel truly wonderful in the hand. This makes them perfect for throws on a sofa or a chair, or as hangings. Those that are not in great shape, or perhaps are even in fragments, may be perfect for cutting up or piecing into pillows. The wealth of options seems infinite. Just to start, there are ikats and suzanis from Uzbekistan, Persian brocades, and the textiles woven for the salwar kameezes and saris from India, which come in such beautiful, saturated hues and shimmer with metallic threads.

I am certainly not a historian, but I am always intrigued to know the history of textiles and the many cultures they come from. The more I learn, the more there is to know. What matters to me above all is how a textile looks and feels: the depth of its colors, the way it reveals its maker's culture through the harmony and poetry of texture, pattern, and palette. These details capture a design's essence. So textiles are my details.

PRECEDING SPREAD, LEFT: A late nineteenth-century Indian skirt richly embroidered in gold. PRECEDING SPREAD, RIGHT: Japanese Meiji period (late 1860s) earthenware vases juxtaposed with a contemporary bronze sculpture. OPPOSITE: A painted fabric scene infuses this Washington, D.C., living room with a mural-like feeling. A nineteenth-century Syrian chandelier adds a delicate filigree of ornament. The back of the period French chaise is upholstered with a fragment of an Aubusson carpet.

RIGHT AND OVERLEAF: In this deep-blue Baltimore dining room, an antique Persian Kerman rug lightens the dark wood floor. Early twentieth-century panels embroidered with plants and animals drape the windows. A mid-nineteenth-century Asian textile runs the length of the mahogany table with a vintage Murano glass chandelier above. A symmetrical arrangement of Donald Sultan engravings, mid-sixteenth-century Spanish tiles, and a George III gilt mirror blend the past with the nearer past above a George III sideboard. In one corner of the room is a seating area with late nineteenth-century French club chairs for intimate dinners for two. The rug is Persian, c. 1920. The glass pendant light is Swedish, c. 1940. The eighteenth-century Chinese two-handled porcelain vase balances the larger Chinese porcelain jug on the dining table.

PRECEDING SPREAD AND ABOVE: In this Washington, D.C., lounge, a custom sectional sofa faces a
French Art Deco zinc bar that we retrofitted for the purpose. French pine-and-iron doors, c. 1880,
front the custom cabinets. An 1860s silk brocade from Persia drapes the sofa back. An old Turkish
Suzani textile used for a pillow cover adds pattern and charm. OPPOSITE: A Persian Kilim Variam
rug, c. 1900, establishes a base of pattern and color for a guest bedroom in a Chevy Chase,
Maryland, home. A nineteenth-century silk suzani drapes over the seat of the French sleigh bed,
c. 1860. An antique Turkish prayer rug adds another layer of texture on top of the ottoman.

RIGHT: An Art Deco silk brocade makes a wonderful face for a velvet-backed pillow cover.
OPPOSITE: A vintage gilt-framed mirror brings a glimmer of reflected light to this powder room. The onyx-topped vanity incorporates an early twentieth-century Regency-style serpentine radiator cover.
OVERLEAF: A mix of period and contemporary elements and modern art give this California guest bedroom a sophisticated yet cozy feeling. The draperies are pieced-together panels of vintage Turkish wool textiles. A nineteenth-century Uzbekistan silk suzani covers the bed with pattern and texture. An early eighteenth-century French side table and an English campaign chest fold in a Continental flavor.

PRECEDING SPREAD, LEFT: Rare ninth-century Arabian bronze camel bells look beautiful against a modern silk velvet. PRECEDING SPREAD, RIGHT: The marriage of ancient and modern, of East and West, creates a timeless place for conversation before and after meals at the far end of a Washington, D.C., dining room. A 1950s cocktail table centers the new upholstered pieces. Standing on the side table is a late seventeenth-century ceramic Turkish Cavetto plate. RIGHT: Because the master bedroom of this Baltimore house is on the top floor, we were able to raise the original 8-foot ceiling plane. Though the room looks monochromatic, antiques, textiles, and art add subtle color without disturbing the calm. In the corner are a late nineteenth-century Napoleon III chaise and a late eighteenth-century European library table. Custom pillow covers incorporate an early twenti-eth-century Turkish Ushak rug. A late nineteenth-century Italian lace and embroidered drapery serves as a coverlet.

ANTIQUE FABRICS ARE ALWAYS
WOVEN OF NATURAL FIBERS.
BECAUSE THEY SOFTEN WITH
AGE, THEY FEEL GOOD AS THROWS
ON SOFAS, CHAIRS, OR BEDS.
THEY LOOK BEAUTIFUL
AS HANGINGS. THOSE THAT
ARE IN NOT GREAT SHAPE CAN
BE PERFECT FOR CUTTING UP
AND MAKING INTO PILLOWS.

RIGHT: In the Baltimore bedroom, a midcentury Adrian Pearsall lounge chair offers a comfortable option for reading and relaxing. A small elm-and-oak chest nearby dates to the late seventeenth century; above it hangs an early twentieth-century mirror from the Middle East. The marble mantel, an English reproduction of an early nineteenth-century original, displays a grouping of tenth-century Persian pottery. OVERLEAF LEFT: A group of Turkish and Persian textiles stored in a cedar closet at the top floor of my design studio; their deep reds and blues will add warmth to any interior. OVERLEAF RIGHT: The abundant natural light of this Washington, D.C., family room makes the rich colors of the Persian textiles feel even richer among all the neutrals. The armchairs date to c. 1920. A pair of mid-nineteenth-century Chinese porcelain vases rest on the side table. A 1930s Turkish carpet sets the tone of the room.

WITH TEXTILES, MORE IS MORE.
WHEN A FABRIC IS HANDMADE,
SOMEONE HAS BROUGHT IT TO
LIFE THROUGH EXPERIENCE.
IT HAS MYSTERY. IT IS EXOTIC.
EVERY SINGLE ONE OF ITS
THREADS HAS AN INTUITION
AND AN INTENT. WHATEVER THE
TEXTILE BECOMES, IT ALWAYS
KEEPS ITS POETRY AND SOUL.

PRECEDING SPREAD, LEFT: A custom pillow made with a seventeenth-century European tapestry looks wonderful to my eye with this modern fabric that reinterprets an old Persian rug. PRECEDING SPREAD, RIGHT: On a covered porch overlooking gardens in Baltimore, a hanging Turkish quilt stands out against the fieldstone walls. An early nineteenth-century Chinese rug drapes a wrought-iron garden bench from the 1880s. A mid-nineteenth-century Persian textile on top of a vintage Turkish wool textile covers the pavers. A white Chinese garden stool and nineteenth- and early twentieth-century painted terra-cotta jars and planters round out the Asian influences. OPPOSITE: Though the color palette of this bedroom is very neutral, layers of textiles make it sumptuous.

RIGHT: A modern carpet provides a foundation for a collection of textiles that includes a rare, late eight-eenth-century hand-embroidered skirt from Goa so delicate it seemed best to frame it. A Bieder-meier cabinet provides additional storage space. An Italian chandelier, c. 1900, sparkles overhead.

IN LAYERING TEXTILES, BUILDING
A SHARED VOCABULARY OF
COLOR, PATTERN, AND TEXTURE
IS ULTIMATELY MUCH MORE
INTERESTING THAN FINDING
THE PERFECT MATCH. THE
GOAL IS TO MARRY SENSUALITY
WITH SENSIBILITY WITH
PERSONALITY. TEXTILES
ACCOMPLISH THAT WITH SUCH
ROMANCE BECAUSE THEY ARE
SOFT, INVITING, AND BEAUTIFUL.

PRECEDING SPREAD, LEFT: In my studio closet, mid-sixteenth-century Flemish verdure tapestry pillows nest with pillows dressed in a variety of antique textiles as well as contemporary fabrics. PRECEDING SPREAD, RIGHT: This San Francisco living room overlooks the Bay, so various shades of blue weave their way into the color palette. A Heriz rug, c. 1920, from northwest Persia establishes the foundation. Custom pillows show off a range of mid-sixteenth-century Flemish verdure tapestries. RIGHT: With a modern white leather Italian sofa, sumptuous blue velvet pillows, and pillows covered in an antique Turkish linen, this family room gives a contemporary twist to the classic blue-and-white color scheme. The paisley curtain fabric—an Indian hand-block print in blue and brown—adds in subtle pattern.

ABOVE AND OPPOSITE: The daughter of this house is young, active, and creative.
She chose the palette of pinks and purples (her favorite colors). We balanced the
bright, warm tones with cool, fresh shades of chartreuse in the curtain fabric.

RIGHT: I love working with young adults. It is exciting to introduce them to interesting pieces from places and eras other than those they know well and create a room they can grow into. This bedroom in Baltimore belongs to the daughter of the house, who chose the pale blue of the walls. The color is a wonderful backdrop for a Danish slant-front secretary chest, c. 1800, a late eighteenth-century Swedish pine table, and a Turkish quilt.

IF YOU CAN FIND AND REFURBISH
AN OLD PIECE TO WORK FOR
TODAY, IT WILL HAVE A SPECIAL
CHARM THAT IS SO ATTRACTIVE.
THE APPEAL IS MORE THAN
JUST A VISCERAL RESPONSE TO
BEAUTY. IT ALSO ENCOMPASSES
FUNCTIONALITY, FOR GOOD
DESIGN INVOLVES BOTH.

OPPOSITE: To make the entry into the pergola of this Washington, D.C., house more appealing, I combined some beautiful but unexpected objects. Nineteenth-century architectural brackets, a late nineteenth-century carved marble column, a mid-nineteenth century Ottoman marble basin, and a late eighteenth-century cast-iron table create a room-like setting out of doors. A Han Dynasty pottery pillar is the piece de resistance.

RIGHT: An understated hand-woven vintage Persian rug, fabric shades with a stripe similar to the rug's, and a nineteenth-century Ottoman Mashrabiya oak panel establish the feeling of this screened porch in Chevy Chase, Maryland. Two contemporary sofas, a pair of midcentury Pierre Jeanneret chairs and an American pine settee, c. 1860, form a welcoming seating arrangement. Knitted mohair and wool pillows add more warmth, texture, and softness.

OVERLEAF: Framed panels of early twentieth-century Indonesian ikat add soul to this enclosed porch. With a Moroccan rug from the 1940s, French wrought-iron armchairs, c. 1880, and nineteenth-century Syrian brass pots, they soften the effect of all the hard surfaces.

FURNISHINGS:
BLENDING ANTIQUE
AND MODERN

I love beautiful things. It does not matter to me how old or new a piece is, or what its style or country of origin may be. Putting together the pieces of room is a very pleasant puzzle. Perhaps it is unusual to believe that an Egyptian mirror fits perfectly with an eighteenth-century English chest of drawers and a 1940s French slipper chair. But there is something to this kind of unexpected arrangement, and to the belief that there is a harmony to be found by blending together furnishings from the entire span of cultures and periods of design in a way that captures the personalities of the people who will be living with them and envelopes them in comfort.

When the ornamentation of a piece is excessive, I tend to shy away. But there is overdone, and overdone. Eighteenth- and nineteenth-century Syrian pieces covered in mother-of-pearl, for example, have a refinement and subtlety that I adore. Even in the complexity of the surface pattern, there are rhyme and reason. Modern designs contrast with and enhance older designs, no matter where they come from, in ways that can surprise, delight, and comfort. Together these pieces from very different places and times can create a beautiful, congenial environment through a combination of forms, colors, and textures. The shapes, the shades of the wood, the hardware, the details—all these considerations factor into how I fit together the elements of a room.

Classic never goes out of style. Old, charming pieces mixed with modern designs capture my heart. Sometimes the perfect antique, vintage, or modern item appears without looking. Sometimes it seems impossible to find the right design, whether old or new, even though the marketplace offers so many wonderful options. If I cannot find what I need in terms of style, size, or look, I will create a custom piece (this is especially true of seating and cabinetry).

RIGHT: In this Washington, D.C., living room, a custom carpet with a Moorish stripe ties together a mix of furnishings that includes Art Deco lounge chairs and a pairing of nineteenth- and early twentieth-century side tables. OVERLEAF: Custom sofas, contemporary chrome-and-leather chairs, a nineteenth-century Italian giltwood chandelier, a Chinese carpet, c. 1930, and bracing modern art create an eclectic array. SECOND OVERLEAF: Form, color, and material can link objects together across time and culture. On the left, the chrome scroll at the base of the chair legs echoes a pattern element in the border of the antique Chinese carpet. On the right, the gilded decoration of a custom coffee table provides a setting for an engraved Persian brass bowl, c. 1850, and an ornate French magnifying glass.

ABOVE: A vignette brings together a late eighteenth-century Asian lacquered gilt table, an antique South Indian metal and silver-wire vase, and nineteenth-century ormolu candlesticks.
OPPOSITE: This early twentieth-century Baltimore house welcomes objects from many different periods and places. The mid-nineteenth-century three-tiered marquetry table holds a late Roman Byzantine censer, an Art Nouveau vase, and a fourteenth-century Peruvian pottery bowl.

My designs are always modern, for I cannot bear replicas. I prefer to search out, rework, and refurbish older pieces rather than attempting to copy something that exists. Pieces with age always have a heart and soul that is much more interesting to me than a custom design or a replica.

But I love modern furniture, especially modern upholstered seating. It is so much more comfortable than vintage or antique seating, although the craftsmanship of pieces with age tends to be so special. For people to use their upholstered seating, it needs to be very inviting. This is especially true of sofas, lounge chairs, and seating around the dining table, and that is why I always incorporate upholstery from our own time. My preference also is for thick, lofty cushioning. Some prefer their upholstery to be very firm. I think, though, that most people want to lounge. And when they sit, they love to feel deeply cocooned into the seating. To be able to specify comfort to such a degree is one of design's greatest benefits.

Individual pieces and their arrangement need to relate to the architecture of the house, and flow nicely within the proportions of the rooms. The furnishings work better when they are appropriate in scale and composition. But I am never literal. It does not do to force a style on a room where it does not feel right. The choices depend on personality and lifestyle, the surroundings, and the light that comes into the space.

I do not design interiors just to look pretty. Pretty is not pretty if it is not comfortable. I love using rooms and everything in them, and I am always pleased when a client makes the most of every piece in every room. Homes are for comfort. And for joy.

RIGHT: The design vocabularies of the early twentieth-century Syrian carved and inlaid mirror, Anglo-Indian console table, and nineteenth-century engraved brass candlestick may be different, but they marry well against white walls. OVERLEAF: The owners of this Chevy Chase, Maryland, residence, fell in love with the late nineteenth-century silk Tabriz rug from Persia. It provides a unifying base for a nineteenth-century Continental fruitwood canape, a nineteenth-century bouillotte lamp, William and Mary-style armchairs, and an early nineteenth-century Swedish pine and lacquered box.

IF YOU CAN FIND AND REFURBISH
AN OLD PIECE TO WORK FOR
TODAY, IT WILL HAVE A SPECIAL
CHARM THAT IS SO ATTRACTIVE.
THE APPEAL IS MORE THAN
JUST A VISCERAL RESPONSE TO
BEAUTY. IT ALSO ENCOMPASSES
FUNCTIONALITY, FOR
GOOD DESIGN INVOLVES BOTH.

PRECEDING SPREAD, LEFT: The sensuously curved frame of the nineteenth-century canape feels at home with the more modest swags of the nineteenth-century table lamp. PRECEDING SPREAD, RIGHT: Flanked by William and Mary–style arm-chairs, the fireplace mantel is a perfect place to display an unexpected grouping of art and objects. Mirrored nineteenth-century Venetian glass sconces frame a c. 1750 engraving, a two-handled flask from Cyprus, 800 BC, and a mid-eighteenth-century Chinese porcelain vase, among other artworks. Below is an early nineteenth-century Swedish pine and lacquered box. RIGHT: Combined with caned Regency chairs, a nineteenth-century Anatolian Ushak, and a framed antique Turkish textile, this French painted cabinet turns the hallway into an interesting, beautiful, and multi-functional destination.

ABOVE: An handmade, inlaid mother-of-pearl Syrian mirror, c. 1940, and a nineteenth-century Syrian chest retrofitted as a vanity make this Annapolis, Maryland, powder room feel very inviting. OPPOSITE: An antique Persian Lever Kerman rug is in keeping with the pale color palette of the living room, where custom sofas are upholstered in luxurious silk velvet and linen. An antique inlaid Syrian chest of drawers draws attention to one of the four corner niches.

IT IS PREFERABLE FOR
INDIVIDUAL PIECES AND THEIR
ARRANGEMENTS TO RELATE TO
THE ARCHITECTURE OF
THE HOUSE AND FIT NICELY
WITHIN THE PROPORTIONS
OF THE ROOMS. FURNISHINGS
AND GROUPINGS TEND TO
WORK BETTER WHEN THEY
ARE APPROPRIATE IN
SCALE AND COMPOSITION.

RIGHT: Early twentieth-century George III–style chairs surround
a nineteenth-century English table in the dining room of the
Annapolis house. George III–style giltwood mirrors enhance the
niches flanking the fireplace. A contemporary abstract painting
above the mantel appeals to the owner, who loves traditional
furnishings leavened by some modern pieces and modern
artwork. OVERLEAF: The intricate pattern of the mother-of-pearl
inlay on this Syrian chest has its own rhyme and reason.
Retrofitted as a vanity with a Calacatta marble counter and
sink, it makes this powder room unique and memorably exotic.

ABOVE: Just adjacent is the lady of the house's dressing room, with an antique inlaid Syrian chest and a French steel-cut mirror, c. 1880. OPPOSITE: With a Biedermeier secretary and late nineteenth-century French giltwood chair, the corner of this Washington, D.C., bedroom becomes a wonderful place to write a note or look at a book. OVERLEAF: The bedroom reveals its great light and views, which drapery modulates and highlights. A combination of lace and silk fabrics speaks to both feminine and masculine aesthetics. Washington tends toward formality; late nineteenth-century French giltwood chairs suggest that attitude.

ABOVE: In a bench and a chair in a master bath, the intricate carving and turned, polished wood of the East is juxtaposed with the painted and gilded wood of the West. OPPOSITE: A mid-nineteenth-century Syrian carved bench adds function and a decorative flourish just outside the shower. Pink glass rondels in the window provide privacy without diminishing the natural light.

IT DOES NOT DO TO FORCE A
PARTICULAR STYLE OR PERIOD
OF DESIGN ON A ROOM WHERE
IT DOES NOT FEEL RIGHT.
WHETHER TRADITIONAL OR
CONTEMPORARY, THE CHOICES
ALWAYS DEPEND ON THE
OWNER'S PERSONALITY,
PREFERENCES, AND LIFESTYLE,
THE ARCHITECTURE, AND
THE WIDER SURROUNDINGS.

OPPOSITE: A Chinese ancestral portrait depicting three generations adds bright color to the neutral palette of this family room and makes a point about shared history. A late nineteenth-century Turkish Sivas rug covers the floor. A tenth-century Persian pottery bowl is a grace note on the coffee table.

RIGHT: In an all-white or almost all-white space such as this master bedroom, different textures, the occasional contrasting dark wood, and a little bit of gilding create interest. Even in such a large space, every corner can be used and enjoyed. Here, a late nineteenth-century Anglo-Colonial linen press provides extra storage.

ABOVE: A basement entertainment/media/family room in a Chevy Chase, Maryland, residence is full of color. Hugging one side of the room, an L-shaped sectional sofa is large enough for the whole family and friends to gather. OPPOSITE: Vladimir Kagan's swivel arm chairs feel happy, optimistic, and futuristic even though the design dates to the 1950s. OVERLEAF: In the gentleman's bath of this historic Washington, D.C., house, a wing chair upholstered in woven leather melds a classic form with an up-to-date material. The original carved mantel stands out against a new, minimal surround.

EVERY SPACE IS A COMPOSITION.
CREATING A PLAN IS LIKE MAKING
A PAINTING. YOU BUILD IT
PIECE BY PIECE. SOMETIMES THE
OVERALL DESIGN COMBINES
VERY MODERN PIECES WITH VERY
TRADITIONAL ANTIQUES.
SOMETIMES IT DOESN'T. THE
PROCESS IS ALWAYS VERY
INSTINCTIVE AND HANDS ON.

OPPOSITE: A nineteenth-century cast-iron garden bench feels appropriate
for this Los Angeles portico, which opens to the grounds and gardens.

ABOVE: The intricate arabesque designs of the hand-carved early twentieth-century Indian chairs, settee, and table add an exotic feeling to the terrace of this house in Chevy Chase, Maryland. OPPOSITE: The decorative motifs of the Indian pieces mirror the hand-chased ornament on the nineteenth-century Asian metal planter, but at different scales. OVERLEAF: A heavy, nineteenth-century hand-embroidered Syrian textile (in red) and a vintage Turkish wool textile serve as rugs on this furnished terrace off the master bedroom of a house in Chevy Chase, Maryland. A cast-brass table with a marble top, c. 1860, pairs with a contemporary glass-top table in front of the sofa.

COLLECTING:
ART AND DECORATIVE
OBJECTS

We who love the history of design and architecture find the idea of restraint—that less is more—to be very compelling and always modern. But I am just as captivated by the continuum of our visual heritage, with its layers upon layers of history and culture. From this point of view, I am enamored with the concept that more is more, and with the complexity that connotes.

Sumptuous rooms—collected rooms—reflect the owners' passions, their lives. When each piece is handmade, the room contains a range of individual experiences because each object expresses something of the heart and soul of its maker. The honesty used in creating the older pieces—this is poetry to me. Above all, I relate to the way beautiful, old things live with those of our time. I love to arrange the more ornate pieces often with very modern, simpler pieces, mixing the strong and subtle so the overall effect is well balanced.

When I am designing a home, I offer the client artworks and objects from all over the world. Much of the porcelain I use is English, from the nineteenth century. I find its shapes, colors, and patterns so pleasing. It feels wonderful to the touch. It lives naturally with other pieces from many different periods and places of origin. I might suggest a small, luminous work by Albert Bierstadt to place nearby. Then I might propose some repoussé Baltimore silver, a bold painting by a contemporary artist, and perhaps an early Tiffany lamp with a rare, unusual silk shade. (I love the Tiffany glass shades also, but the silk ones are charming in their simplicity, and also very different than what we usually find.) I am not one to organize things or group items into strict categories. Nor do I feel that fine pieces must only keep company with fine pieces.

OPPOSITE: Shades of deep blue help to create intimacy in this wood-paneled Baltimore study. The little carpet, which was too fragile for the floor, adds beauty to the wall. OVERLEAF: Whenever I find objects and furnishings that interest me, I purchase the pieces. Sometimes I have a specific client in mind. Sometimes I know I'll find the right place for them later, and I arrange them in my studio in the meantime.

ABOVE: Objects from many different eras and countries come together in my studio. An early twentieth-century bookcase holds a Persian tile with hunting scene, c. 1880. In the corner is a nineteenth-century Japanese lacquered screen. OPPOSITE: On one wall of an Annapolis dining room, a nineteenth-century screen, William and Mary stool, a mid-eighteenth-century English mahogany sideboard, and tenth-century Persian pottery bowl contribute to a fascinating marriage of periods, cultures, and styles. OVERLEAF: In my home, glass vitrines house my collection of eleventh- to thirteenth-century Persian, Syrian, Turkish, and Asian pottery pieces. One of my favorite pieces is a two-handle Messapian amphora dating to c. 400 BC.

In all the ancient cultures, artworks and craftsmanship from the period between the eighth and ninth century through the twelfth century captures my imagination. The pottery never stops amazing me, whether it comes from China, Japan, Persia, Egypt, or elsewhere. I particularly love to introduce my clients to the pottery from the Mediterranean countries. Its simplicity is remarkable. So is its straightforwardness. The patterns always incorporate calligraphy, so the surface ornamentation means something. And the pots themselves tend to look so very modern.

Metalwork is another part of the vocabulary of design development the world over, and so often how we think of cultures in progress: an Iron Age, a Bronze Age, a Golden Age. Through the mosque lamp, for example, we can trace a path of illumination around the globe. The basic design—a very simple globe etched with calligraphy, both art and expression—emerged in the sixth century. In the centuries since, so many cultures have emulated the form, adapting it over and over again to different eras and contexts. In this way, it has become a part of an international vocabulary. So many variations on the original still exist in the market today—a true artistic development.

These artisans of the past were masters of their arts. I cannot help but honor them. Nameless though they remain, they have shaped so much of my sensibility. I marvel at how much beauty they left for us to discover and cherish. The tiles. The pottery. The copper plates and cups. The lanterns. The textiles. The rugs. Grouped in collections and placed carefully, each individual piece enhances the others and creates an indescribable feeling of another time and place. The colors are peerless. The naivete of some of the designs is breathtaking. The spontaneity of some of the pieces is unmatched. Each and every one has a heart and soul. Every single piece was created for a purpose. And every single piece is an expression of the art of its maker.

OPPOSITE: In this Los Angeles living room, the formal balances the informal and the rustic balances the refined. Because the room is awash in natural light, we chose a pale color palette. The fireplace mantel is antique. Instead of a painting or a mirror, I hung a collection of Islamic polychromatic footed bowls with and eleventh- and twelfth-century Persian bowls. OVERLEAF, RIGHT: Late-nineteenth-century Japanese panels create a natural background for a grouping of Asian vases. OVERLEAF, LEFT: The dark wood of this Syrian corner cabinet provides a rich backdrop for tenth-century ceramic bowls.

THE ARTISANS OF THE PAST
WERE MASTERS OF THEIR ARTS.
I CANNOT HELP BUT HONOR
THEM. NAMELESS THOUGH THEY
REMAIN, THEY HAVE SHAPED
SO MUCH OF MY SENSIBILITY.
I MARVEL AT HOW MUCH
BEAUTY THEY LEFT FOR US TO
DISCOVER AND CHERISH.

PRECEDING SPREAD: To refresh the living room in this century-old Baltimore house, we painted everything white and blended European pieces with objects and art from Asia and the Middle East. Late nineteenth-century Japanese panels flank the windows. A Chinese lacquer glazed table, c. 1600, sits in front of the sofa. A late nineteenth-century European embroidered silk textile drapes over the hassock. OPPOSITE AND OVERLEAF: English, Persian, and Flemish antiques from different eras feel at home in this Chevy Chase, Maryland, living room. Bordered by a collection of Persian and Turkish pottery, a mid-seventeenth-century Flemish tapestry transforms the space over the sofa. A late George III leather trunk serves as a coffee table.

PRECEDING SPREAD, LEFT: The pattern language of this pottery bowl is an example of Mudejar design, a Moorish- or Islamic-influenced style that developed in Spain before the fifteenth century. PRECEDING SPREAD, RIGHT: A late seventeenth-century Dutch oak table takes center stage in this Baltimore kitchen addition. RIGHT: Saturated shades of blue enliven this serene San Francisco living room. Flanked by nineteenth-century giltwood sconces, an English bookcase, c. 1810, displays the client's collection of porcelain and decorative objects. A Tabriz carpet, c. 1900, from northwest Persia covers the floor. A late nineteenth-century French parcel-gilt chandelier floats turquoise accents overhead.

THE WAY BEAUTIFUL, OLD
THINGS CAN LIVE WITH THOSE
OF OUR TIME IS SO FASCINATING.
THE DESIGN CHALLENGE COMES
IN BLENDING THE MORE ORNATE
ANTIQUES WITH THE MODERN,
SIMPLER PIECES. WHEN THE
STRONG AND THE SUBTLE ARE
WELL BALANCED, THE OVERALL
EFFECT IS COMPLETE HARMONY.

OPPOSITE AND OVERLEAF: The owners of this Chevy Chase, Maryland, residence had a wonderful piece of Roman sculpture they wanted to display on high in their dining room. I designed a simple, modern base for it accordingly. In contrast, the bold geometric decoration of a handled vessel dating to 350 AD is a foil to the inlaid marble top of a Victorian lamp table.

ABOVE: The nineteenth-century ormolu candlesticks feel just right in combination with a drawing by Allan D'Arcangelo. OPPOSITE: We opened up the main entry of this Washington, D.C., house to create a welcoming view through to the backyard while keeping the flavor of the original architecture. In each room and every transitional space, antiques mix with modern pieces and contemporary artwork. *Square Primaries and Secondaries*, a set of six silkscreens by D. Brown, makes a dramatic statement on the stair landing.

WHEN COMBINING ARTWORKS
AND OBJECTS FROM ALL OVER
THE WORLD, IT IS MORE
INTERESTING TO ARRANGE
PIECES SO THAT THEY FEEL
RIGHT TOGETHER RATHER
THAN ORGANIZING THEM INTO
STRICT CATEGORIES. FINE
PIECES CAN ALWAYS KEEP
COMPANY WITH FINE PIECES,
BUT THEY WORK BEAUTIFULLY
WITH EVERYDAY ITEMS, TOO.

PRECEDING SPREAD, LEFT: A bird's-eye view from the top of the stairs in the Baltimore brownstone that is home to my design studio. PRECEDING SPREAD, RIGHT: I love English porcelain for its feel and its beautiful sheen. Many of the pieces find a temporary place in my studio until I find them the perfect home. OPPOSITE AND OVERLEAF: A vintage Murano chandelier casts a soft lilac glow into this deep-blue Baltimore dining room. A sixteenth-century Chinese porcelain jar provides a centerpiece for a nineteenth-century Regency-style mahogany dining table laid with a fabric fragment from a Yomud tent. A late nineteenth-century pine-and-gesso mantel displays an early twentieth-century French cameo vase, a mid-eighteenth-century Chinese porcelain bubble vase, and a Persian molded tile, c. 1850.

THE EFFECT OF LAYERING IN A
ROOM IS SO SUMPTUOUS. THE
DIFFERENT ITEMS REFLECT
PEOPLE'S LIVES, THEIR INTERESTS,
TRAVELS, AND COLLECTIONS.
WHATEVER THEY ARE, WHEN
THEY ARE HANDMADE THEY
HAVE POETRY AND A SOUL
BECAUSE SOMEONE HAS BROUGHT
THEM INTO BEING THROUGH
THEIR OWN EXPERIENCE.

OPPOSITE AND OVERLEAF: In this dining room in Washington, D.C., the top of the
commode is home to a collection of art and objects that spans the ancient
world to the twentieth century. A Biedermeier side chair sits voluptuously in
front of a late nineteenth-century Kermanshah fragment of a Shahsavan panel
from northwest Iran. The rug is an early twentieth-century Persian Karaja.
On the other side of the room, a hexagonal Continental vase and a Chinese
black and gilt lacquer sofa table, c. 1840, continue the decorative language.

MORE DOWN-TO-EARTH
COLLECTIONS ARE JUST AS
EXCITING TO ASSEMBLE AND
WORK WITH AS FINE ARTWORKS
BECAUSE THEIR VALUE IS SO
PERSONAL. THERE IS SUCH GREAT
CHARM AND MEANING WITH
PIECES THAT ARE COLLECTED
THROUGH TRAVEL OR BECAUSE
OF A PARTICULAR PASSION.

PRECEDING SPREAD: With piles of books and so many other beloved and unique objects, this formal Chevy Chase, Maryland, living room has a relaxed, collected feel. OPPOSITE: By framing these British photographs of houses and interiors in the same style and grouping them together, the collection becomes a narrative, a graphic tale defined by its subject matter.

THERE IS NOTHING MORE EXOTIC
THAN ROOMS AND HOMES THAT
MIX ITEMS FROM THE EAST
AND THE WEST. BLENDING THE
DIFFERENT ELEMENTS IS A VERY
PLEASANT AND INTERESTING
CHALLENGE. IT DOESN'T MATTER
HOW OLD OR NEW THE
PIECES ARE. WHAT MATTERS IS
THAT THEY ARE BEAUTIFUL.

PRECEDING SPREAD: When we renovated this house, the main portion of the working kitchen became the back section of a larger area. The two flow naturally into one another. Rugs and a collection of kitchen implements from the late eighteenth century give this working space the feel of a room.

OPPOSITE: To make the family room addition to this old Baltimore house feel true to the original, we incorporated stone walls like those visible elsewhere in the structure. In one corner, a late nineteenth-century giltwood mirror anchors a wall grouping that includes a pairing of glazed Portuguese pottery bowls, c. 1900, a nineteenth-century Continental corner chair, a nineteenth-century rosewood side table, and a late nineteenth-century Persian Bidjar rug.

RIGHT: With objects, textiles, and furnishings from different periods and places, this newly added room feels as if it has existed for some time. A lyrical Elger Esser photograph hangs over one length of the L-shaped sofa, while a suzani draped over the back of the other adds a layer of pattern and texture. A Turkish Ushak, c. 1900, warms the floor.

IF IT FEELS GOOD,
IT IS GOOD

For me, good design is a marriage of architecture and interiors. I do not believe there are formulas for designing spaces. This does not mean there are no rules. It makes sense to have a base, a foundation of practicalities. When I am designing spaces, my intent is focused on the comfort of things, on circulation, and on beauty. That is why when we draw a plan, I always tell the homeowners it will change. And more often than not, it does.

One can have the most beautiful room, but if the architecture is lacking, there are limitations. I look at the surroundings, the light, the client's way of living. Then I build the room in my mind like a painting. The process is instinctive, not intellectual, and hands on. How many people will sit in the space? What extras will they need? What about side tables, coffee tables, and lighting. The lighting is extremely important, because where and what I highlight sets the mood. The walls are just as critical, and the colors, too.

Traditional homes often have traditional furniture. I shy away from such a look. Suppose the dining room of a nineteenth-century house still has all its original casings, trim, and molding in place. But it also has all extra ornament that people have added to it over the years. If I find the original beautiful, I will keep it place. But I will inevitably edit and clean up the extra. I would probably center the room on a very modern, extendable table—functionality to me is very modern—and surround it with comfortable, contemporary chairs. My initial instinct might be to cover the chair seats in some unexpected, exotic fabric. I might also place a side cabinet from

OPPOSITE: Hanging an intricate eighteenth-century gilt mirror on a nineteenth-century embossed leather screen softens the corner. OVERLEAF: I love combining artworks from different periods, and I have no problem mixing metals and metallic finishes. Here an eighteenth-century giltwood Italian mirror balances a nineteenth-century Russian brass lamp and a contemporary giltwood console table in front of silvery grisaille wallpaper. A nineteenth-century Chinese vase, a seventeenth-century Chinese glazed bowl, an antique Islamic footed bowl, and a Legras floral vase layer into the mix. A Neolithic Majiyao jar and a scalloped brass tray sit underneath the console table.

today on one wall with an antique cabinet opposite. The art would likely incorporate modern works, bold or subtle, with some simpler pieces, perhaps a textile or two, to soften the effect. I might also hang a combination of old, beautiful tiles juxtaposed with some extremely modern plates. In this way, the room becomes a kind of play on periods, styles, and countries of origin. When everything is in place, my goal for it is to create an experience that the hosts and the guests find inviting and enveloping—and that makes them smile and linger through dinner.

In my view, pieces need to relate, but they do not have to match. Think about the walls that flank a window. When they are very symmetrical, the instinct is to make both sides the same. If you can only find one piece of art, the two walls become a dilemma. It would be nicer, of course, if they were exactly alike, but this is when it is important to remember that symmetry is not the only solution. I might hang a beautiful work of modern art on one side. On the other, I might arrange a collection of prints, or works of art that are not traditional, but that still are art. I like to feel the components of the room have been collected over time. A room feels more livable to me that way.

I am certainly blessed to be able to do what I love in my life—and just like in real life, to follow no formulas.

OPPOSITE AND OVERLEAF: Glazed Persian pottery from the eleventh and thirteenth centuries and mid-sixteenth-century Spanish tiles bring pops of brilliant color to carved wood mantel in this Washington, D.C., dining room. This expansive room can accommodate two dining tables, perfect for large dinners as well as more intimate gatherings. We introduced streamlined, modern upholstered chairs for comfort and scale.

PRECEDING SPREAD: The dining room had beautiful original architectural details, but it was very dark when the clients purchased the house. Painting and glazing the walls a neutral green helped to instill a modern spirit. We custom made a drapery from a nineteenth-century Turkish textile with gold thread to curtain the back edge of the early nine-teenth-century English mahogany side-board. An American quilt hangs on the wall above, a unique setting for a small landscape by Albert Bierstadt. RIGHT: This gentleman's study in Baltimore belongs to a veterinarian who photographs animals when he travels the world. We honored his passions by enlarging, framing, and hanging his photographs gallerystyle to cover the walls. A Persian Bakshaish carpet, c. 1880, helps to establish the room's color palette and pattern language.

PRECEDING SPREAD: Three
early nineteenth-century
dignitaries by Robert
Lefevre cast their watchful
eyes over this Los Angeles
master bedroom. AKerman
carpet from south central
Persia, c. 1900, harmonizes with the luminous
quality of the natural light.
RIGHT: A midcentury
sideboard retrofitted as a
vanity brings glamour to
this master bathroom in
Los Angeles. Adding to the
room's happy spirit are an
early twentieth-century
George III–style gilt mirror,
a mirrored dressing table,
and a Regency-style
side table from the 1940s.

ABOVE: Along one side of this family room, acrylic nesting tables cozy up to a mid-nineteenth-century Indo-Portuguese settee. A large cityscape by Elger Esser dominates the wall. OPPOSITE; This powder room is part of an addition to a turn-of-the-twentieth-century house in Baltimore. A Turkish marble basin and an eighteenth-century American chest retrofitted for the vanity reflect the client's love of travel.

RIGHT: The focal point of this living room is its spectacular view of San Francisco Bay and Alcatraz, which profoundly influenced the color palette. Two Swedish fauteuils and a late eighteenth-century tea table transform the window bay into an intimate room within a room.

ABOVE, OPPOSITE, AND OVERLEAF: In this Chevy Chase, Maryland, family room, a Sarouk Fereghan carpet from north Persia, c. 1910, lays an underpinning of pattern into the rich, serene space. A Jean Royere sconce harmonizes with midcentury modern furnishings, including an Italian floor lamp and an Arne Jacobsen Egg chair, with furnishings and objects from other times and places. The view to the exterior is so beautiful that we decided to make the room dark to enhance the effect. A pair of late-nineteenth-century French fauteuils add a splash of color picked up by the pillows.

ABOVE AND OPPOSITE: With the exception of the French mirrors, c. 1920, every element of this renovated Washington, D.C., bathroom is a custom design. OVERLEAF: The indoor/outdoor experience essential to the Los Angeles lifestyle. Our goal is always to create outdoor rooms with all the comforts and beauty we expect indoors. In this pool portico, a vintage wrought-iron garden bench establishes one perimeter. A pair of Spanish doors flanking the eighteenth-century limestone fireplace mantel add layers of texture and history.

RIGHT: A late seventeenth-century Dutch table is the perfect scale for this Baltimore kitchen addition designed with reclaimed materials to harmonize with the original house. A mid-twentieth-century lantern feels ethereal even as it marries proportionally with the table. An early twentieth-century Lebanese woven rug acts as a spatial connector.

OVERLEAF: This Washington, D.C., basement used to be dark and compartmentalized. Removing the walls and introducing a neutral palette and vivid paintings by Ken Tate has transformed it into a hangout area for the family's children and their friends.

A BEAUTIFUL, COMFORTABLE,
FUNCTIONAL HOME IS ALWAYS
A MARRIAGE OF ARCHITECTURE
AND INTERIORS. THERE ARE
NO REAL FORMULAS FOR
GOOD DESIGN. BUT THERE
ARE RULES THAT PROVIDE
A BASE FOR COMFORT AND A
FOUNDATION FOR THE
PRACTICALITIES OF LIVING.

OPPOSITE AND OVERLEAF: The architecture of this porch addition to a
Baltimore house creates a natural setting for furnishings that combine
the rustic and the refined. We divided the space, which runs the
length of the house, into distinct areas for different functions and group
sizes. In the dining space, a Moroccan brass tray with concentric bands
of motifs anchors the wall. Two seating areas are perfect for small
gatherings or for one person to sit and contemplate the garden view.
A semi-antique Mediterranean painted table by R. Kime contrasts happily
with a deep wicker sofa laden with pillows. Nineteenth-century French
country terra-cotta jars filled with leafy branches add more rustic notes.

ACKNOWLEDGMENTS

This book—*The Romance of East and West*—has been building up over many years of travel and inspirations that I have carried in my heart and later expressed in the projects I work on. I am thrilled to have so many colleagues and friends who have worked with me to achieve it.

I am happy and thankful for my clients to have invited me into their houses and trusted me in the design of their interiors.

Nicole Adcock makes every project possible. For all of our ups and downs, she's always smiling and keeping the sanity in the building.

I am thankful for Elva Suarez, who keeps our interiors neat and happy.

Ron Czajka, the generous, giving, and brilliant architect, is always there for me, by my side, helping with the excavating.

Debra Potter, who keeps the wheels turning so I can do what I love, design.

Elizabeth White, my editor, has been very sensitive and very kind every step of the way. Thank you to Monacelli Press for making such a commitment to this book.

My thanks to the consummate professional Jill Cohen, who has been instrumental in helping me bring my vision for this book into reality.

Doug Turshen and Steve Turner have been understanding, easy to work with, and so thoughtful in deciphering the intricacies of my vision and bringing them onto the page.

Judith Nasatir has been supportive as we worked together to find language that was close to my voice and my ideas.

For the incredible photographers who have turned their keen eyes and cameras to the rooms in this book, I am so appreciative: Pieter Estersohn, Erik Kvalsvik, Aaron Leitz, Roger Davies.

When I met William Abranowicz, I had a sense of immediate connection. I also experienced something I'd never felt before, that he captured the soul of my work through his lens. I am so grateful, Bill, for your remarkable photographs. You truly inspire me.

I am grateful and blessed with my three loving children Ahmad, Bana, and Walid, who every single day bring light and joy into my life.

Above all, God, the most merciful, the most loving, thank you for the gift of life.

PHOTOGRAPHY CREDITS

William Abranowicz: 1, 2-3, 4-5, 6, 11, 12-13, 16-17, 18-19, 24-25, 64-65, 67, 68-69, 70-71, 77, 78-79, 81, 82-83, 86-87, 92-93, 94-95, 100, 103, 109, 112-13, 116-17, 118-19, 120-21, 124-25, 136-37, 140-41, 146-47, 148, 149, 152-53, 154-55, 157, 158-59, 160, 162-63, 166-67, 170, 172-73, 174-75, 179, 180-81, 184-85, 188-89, 191, 192-93, 194-95, 197, 205, 206-7, 209, 210-11, 212-13

Roger Davies: 21, 29, 30-31, 33, 34-35, 38-39, 40-41, 52-53, 84-85, 151, 165, 216-17, 218-19, 230-31

Pieter Estersohn: 14, 22-23, 26-27, 28, 45, 46-47, 50-51, 55, 56-57, 61, 63, 74-75, 76, 88-89, 91, 97, 98-99, 104-5, 106-7, 110-11, 123, 144-45, 168-69, 187, 201, 202-3, 214-15, 220-21, 224-25, 226-27, 228-29, 232-33, 243-35, 237, 238-39

Eric Kvalsik: 73, 80, 115, 130-31, 132-33, 138-39, 143, 161, 182-83, 198-99

Aaron Leitz: 20, 36-37, 42-43, 48-49, 58-59, 101, 176-77, 222-23

Copyright © 2019 Mona Hajj and The Monacelli Press
Photographs copyright © 2019 William Abranowicz

First published in the United States by The Monacelli Press.
All rights reserved.

Library of Congress Control Number: 2018967521
ISBN: 978-1580935470

Design: Doug Turshen and Steve Turner
Printed in China

The Monacelli Press
6 West 18th Street, suite 2C
New York, New York 10011

ENDPAPERS: Nineteenth-century Turkish, Persian, and Syrian textiles from Mona Hajj's collection.

PAGE 1: A mélange of furniture in Mona Hajj's studio: an early nineteenth-century Dutch screen between a mid-nineteenth-century English bureau bookcase, left, and a contemporary cabinet. In front are an English carved cane bench, c. 1850, and a European fruitwood settee from the 1820s.

PAGES 2-3: A late nineteenth-century embroidered Indian skirt hangs over a silk Tabriz carpet from 1880.

PAGE 4: A late sixteenth-century Italian painted and gilded chest.

PAGE 6: Mid-sixteenth-century Spanish tiles and turquoise-glazed Persian pottery from the eleventh and thirteenth centuries.